YOUR Workbook

Verne Wheelwright, Ph.D.

**A Step-by-Step Guide to YOUR Future
for use with**

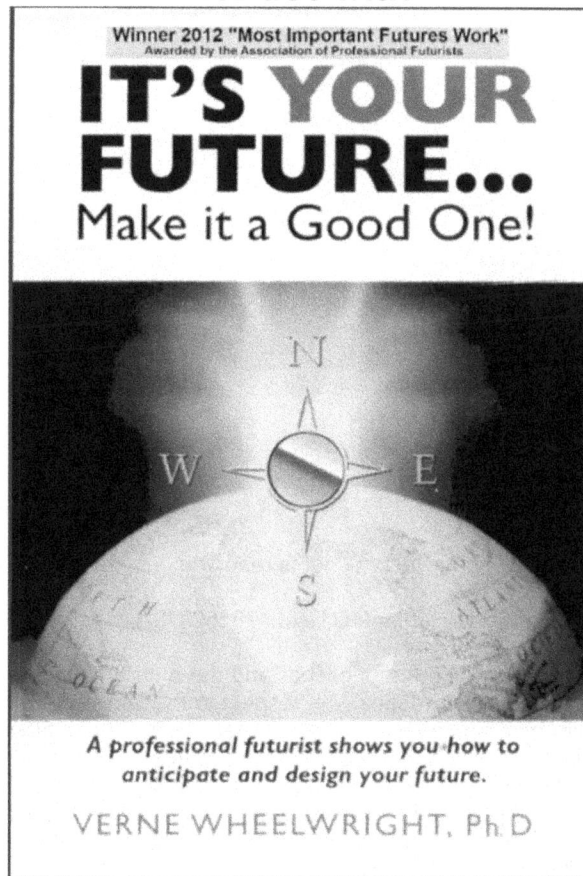

Winner 2012 "Most Important Futures Work"
Awarded by the Association of Professional Futurists

IT'S YOUR FUTURE...
Make it a Good One!

A professional futurist shows you how to
anticipate and design your future.

VERNE WHEELWRIGHT, Ph.D

**Winner of the APF 2012
"Most Important Futures Work"**

Published by the Personal Futures Network, Harlingen, Texas 78552 USA www.personalfutures.net.

Contact:

The Personal Futures Network, 1917 Guava Circle, Harlingen TX 78552
   Telephone: (956) 423-5758   Email: verne@personalfutures.net .Printed in USA

Contents

Your Workbook

There is a lot you can know about your future. More important, there is a lot you can <u>do</u> about your future. You don't have to just let the future happen to you, you can make choices and take actions that will change or determine your future.

This **Personal Futures Workbook** is designed to be used with my award winning book **It's YOUR Future... Make it a Good One!** These two books are written to help you learn about, think about, and plan for your personal future. The book will show you how to use the same methods that professional futurists use in large organizations worldwide, but scaled down to fit you and your family.

This Workbook will lead you step-by-step as you explore the next ten years or more of your life. You will look at your present life, learn about the forces of change that will affect you, consider major events in your future, and define your personal values. Then you will explore your future with scenarios, short stories about what *may* happen in your future.

Finally, you will make decisions about what you want your future to be, then develop strategies and a plan to achieve that future.

Thousands of people all over the world have used this workbook, whether on their own, in classrooms, or in workshops. Many have told me their lives have been changed, and in several cases I have seen that happen.

To learn more about Personal Futures, please visit the web site <u>www.personalfutures.net</u>. To learn more about my books, workshops and presentations, please visit <u>www.vernewheelwright,com.</u> For updates about personal futuring, follow me on Twitter (@urfuturist) or on the Personal Futures Network page on Facebook.

Verne Wheelwright

verne@personalfutures.net

Introduction

What is a personal future? As we interpret personal futures here, they are explorations of the potential futures of one individual, but only the futures that directly involve that individual. You will be learning about the futures that relate directly to *you* and your family.

You will be using the same methods that have been practiced by futurists for decades all over the world. At the end of this process you should have an overview and a vision for your life, specific plans for the next stage of life, and contingency plans to deal with unexpected changes.

What should you be able to expect from studying about your future? The approach you will take with this workbook consists of three steps:

Look at Your Life and Where You Are Now
Life stages
Personal domains and driving forces
Life events
Your values, strengths and weaknesses

Explore Your Futures with Scenarios
Develop a scenario matrix
Examine the driving forces in your life
Create four scenarios

Create Your Future—The Future You Want to Live
Create a vision for the next stage of your life.
Develop strategies
Develop action plans
Develop contingency plans

And the final step..... *Live your plan!*

Section I

Before you can apply futures methods to your life, you must have a base of information from which to draw conclusions about your possible futures. In this section, you will learn about

> 1) the stages of life
> 2) six personal domains that contain the forces that propel life foreword
> 3) life events that can be anticipated, both as to probability of occurrence and extent of impact.

This section will conclude with an examination of your personal values, strengths and weaknesses. This information will become the foundation from which you will create personal scenarios in Section Two.

Stages of life
(Chapter 2 in It's YOUR Future...)

Ten stages of life.

On the next few pages are listed ten life stages, with a very brief description of each stage. As you learn about the stages, be aware of the *change periods between stages*. These transitions are important and sometimes difficult times in your life, but preparation and understanding will help you deal with them. Note that after age sixty, the stages are no longer related to chronological age, but are more related to physical and mental health.

Change is what studying the future is all about. Without change, every day would be like the movie *Groundhog Day* in which every day was the same. When you explore the future, you should be looking for the changes that may (or will) occur in your life.

The descriptions of each life stage are intended to help you think about these stages in terms of images. Hopefully they will trigger mental images of your own that will help you visualize future life stages.

Characteristics of Life Stages

Infant	Birth through 2 years. Dependent. Brain and sensory abilities developing. Learning motor skills.
Child	3-9 years. Growing and mastering motor skills and language. Learning to play and socialize. Continued growth, formal school, and organized activities.
Adolescent	10-19 years. Growth spurts. Puberty brings hormonal changes and reactions. Strong emotions often rule decisions. Risks for injury, alcohol, drugs, tobacco, etc. In some societies or segments, education ends and career, marriage, and family decisions are made.
Young Adult	20-29 years, Completing higher education and beginning career and family. Potential coping and financial pressures
Adult	30-39 years. Managing family and career growth. Increasing numbers of couples are starting families in this stage. Continued coping pressures.
Middle age	40-60 First signs of aging and effects of lifestyle; menopause, children are leaving the nest, grandchildren arrive. Career peak. Aging parents may require help.
Independent Elder	Age 60 onward. More signs of aging and lifestyle effects. Eligible for Social Security, Medicare (U.S.), pensions. Retirement. More discretionary time and opportunities for travel, hobbies and sports. Some health problems and medications. May be caring for a spouse or others. This stage is becoming the longest stage of life.

Vulnerable Elder	Beginning frailty, cognitive or multiple health problems. Require some assistance. Unable to drive. Possible move to Assisted Living facility. This stage is optional, but in the past was the image of old age.
Dependent Elder	Requires daily care. Unable to perform all personal functions. Possible move to a nursing home. This stage is also optional.
End of Life (Up to six months)	Diagnosed with terminal condition or the final stage of a disease. May require hospice care, hospitalization or nursing home care. This stage may be very brief.

Now, look back at the stages of life for a moment. Do you have an image in your mind that describes each life stage? Using the stages and the images, can you see forward to future stages of your life?

To complete the life stages portion of your personal research, decide which life stage you are going to plan for. You can plan for a life stage or you can simply plan for the next ten years.

My present life stage is	
The life stage for my personal strategic plan is	
This life plan ends in the year	

The People in Your Future

Which life stage are you in now? Your children? Your parents? What is the next stage for each of you? Understanding the life stages of family members and other stakeholders helps you prepare for the changes in their lives and for the resulting impacts on your life.

Using the chart on the next page, enter your present age in the first column on the line for the current year, then write in your age for each succeeding year. For the life stage you are in at the present, determine what year that stage ends. Circle that year and enter your age during that year. When does the next stage end? Underline or circle that year as well.

Do the same for each family member. Determine which life stage each person is in now, and in what year that stage will end. When you complete the chart, you will have marked the important life changes for the members of your family, the times when you and each family member change from one life stage to another, and your ages at that time. By reading across the chart, you can relate the changes in family members' lives to your own age and the calendar year.

Note: There is an Excel spreadsheet that simplifies this process and can store *lots* of people and information. It's a free download at **www.personalfutures.net.**

Family members: Ages and Stages

Year	Your age	Spouse age	Oldest child	Youngest child	Oldest parent	Others	Others
Name							
2010							
2011							
2012							
2013							
2014							
2015							
2016							
2017							
2018							
2019							
2020							
2021							
2022							
2023							
2024							
2025							
2026							
2027							
2028							
2029							
2030							
2031							
2032							
2033							
2034							
2035							

For columns headed "Others", list other close friends, family members, or important people in your life. These may vary, depending on your age. You can list grandparents, grandchildren, siblings, close friends, and even pets. An example of a completed worksheet is shown on the next page.

Year	Your age	Spouse age	Oldest grandparent	Youngest grandparent	Oldest parent	Youngest parent	Youngest sister
Name	Chris	Not yet!	Norman	Gert	John	Rhonda	Erin
2010	20		70	60	44	42	18
2011	Young		Independent	Independent	Middle	Middle	Adol
2012	Adult				Age	Age	Young
2013							Adult
2014							
2015							
2016							
2017							
2018							
2019							
2020	30		80	70			
2021	Adult						
2022							30 Adult
2023							
2024							
2025							
2026					60		
2027					Independent		
2028						60	
2029						Ind	
2030	40		90	80			
2031	Middle						
2032	Age						40 mid
2033							
2034					69	66	

Personal Domains
(Chapters 4, 5, 6 in *It's YOUR Future...*)

Personal domains are made up of the forces and sub-forces that move through your life, and, in many cases, move you. When these forces pressure you or motivate you, they are driving forces in your life. Here, we recognize six categories of forces that are common to all people and are a part of every person's life from birth through death.

Each domain may contain several different forces, and any one of these forces may be dominant during a life stage. For example, the Social Domain is usually a driving force in the lives of young adults. In the early years of this stage, time with friends is very important, but when a person makes a decision to marry and start a family, the family now dominates the Social Domain, driving many of the individual's decisions.

Whether with family or friends, this stage tends to be strongly related to the *people* in a person's life, the Social Domain. At the same time, young adults are completing their education and beginning their careers, both forces within the Activities Domain. In the Young Adult stage, the Social (family and friends) and Activities (education and career) domains are often the driving forces in an individual's life.

The Financial Domain may become a more dominant force in the Adult stage, partly due to the needs and demands of the family and partly as the individual finds a need to accumulate savings and assets.

The Health Domain becomes dominant later in life, usually during the Independent stage and the later stages. Younger people may find this domain to be a strong force if they have health problems or a strong focus on diet or physical fitness.

The Housing Domain emerges at different times in life, whenever a concern about acquiring, changing or improving one's housing situation occurs. A need or decision to relocate to a different area also gives this domain temporary importance. Once the needs are satisfied, the Housing Domain recedes into the background.

The Transportation Domain is important to Adolescents as they become eligible to become licensed to drive vehicles, to anyone commuting to work, and again to older people who face the loss of the ability to drive. In some cultures, where few people own automobiles, walking, motorcycles and buses are prominent means of transportation. For most people, little thought is given to transportation until, for some reason, it is not available.

Personal Domains

Activities Domain- All the things you do. For example:

School- training, self-improvement, education throughout your life.
Work or career
Religion
Sports, hobbies, travel, games and entertainment

Finances Domain- Everything related to your finances. For example:

Income, assets
Expense, debt, liabilities
Investments
Financial risks, insurance

Health Domain- Everything related to your health. For example:

Health status- physical and mental condition.
Medications
Diet and exercise
Medical care- care you receive from professionals
Personal care – the help you receive with the activities of living

Housing Domain- Everything related to your home and where you live. For example:

Home- house, apartment, mobile home, care facility
Community your neighborhood and community
Nation, the country where you live
Climate

Social Domain- Everything to do with people in your life. For example:

Family, friends
Co-workers, community
Advisors
Organizations

Transportation Domain- Everything to do with mobility and access. For example

Mobility- walking, wheelchair, scooter
Personal transportation- automobile, bicycle, motorcycle
Distance to commute- to work, markets, health care, etc.
Local public transportation- bus, taxi, local train, ambulance
Long distance public transportation- train, airplane, ship

(Chapter 5 in It's YOUR Future...)

Create a time series and a trend line

For each domain, you can use a chart like the one below to rank the quality of that domain in your life at each age. Using the graphs on the Domain pages that follow, and following the examples below, your first step is to make a line in the box for each ten-year age group, ranking the quality level of your life at that age, up to your present age. Now connect all the lines, creating a line from birth to your current age.

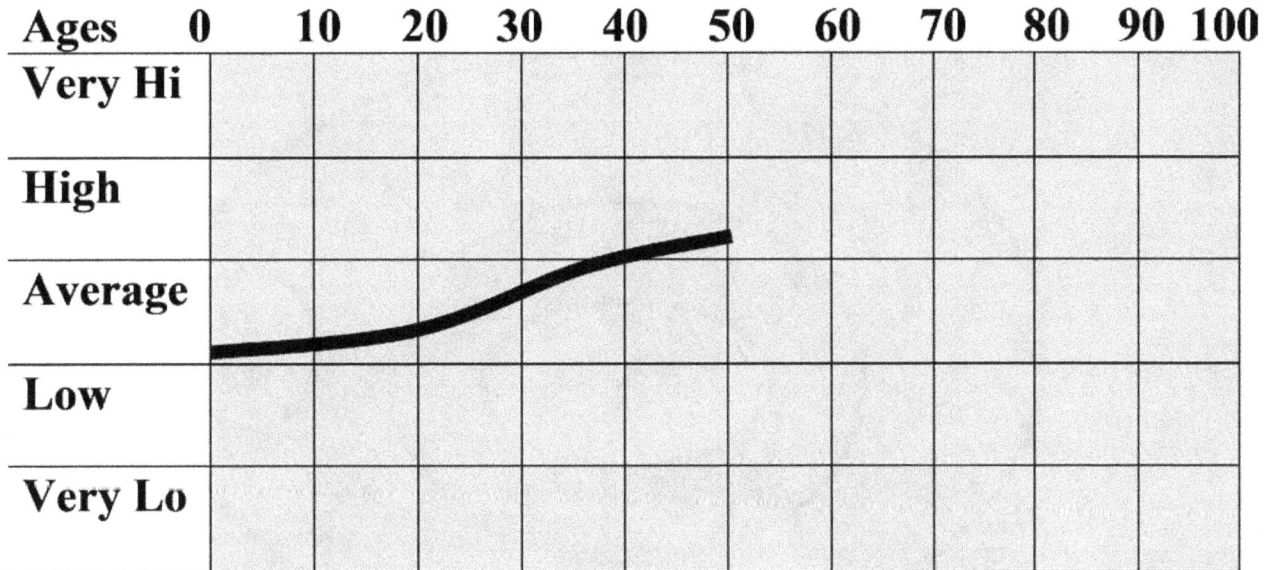

Ages	0	10	20	30	40	50	60	70	80	90	100
Very Hi											
High											
Average											
Low											
Very Lo											

Next, project one line into the future stage you plan to study, as seen below. This line will represent your best estimation of the highest plausible quality for the next life stage. This is your optimistic projection for this domain.

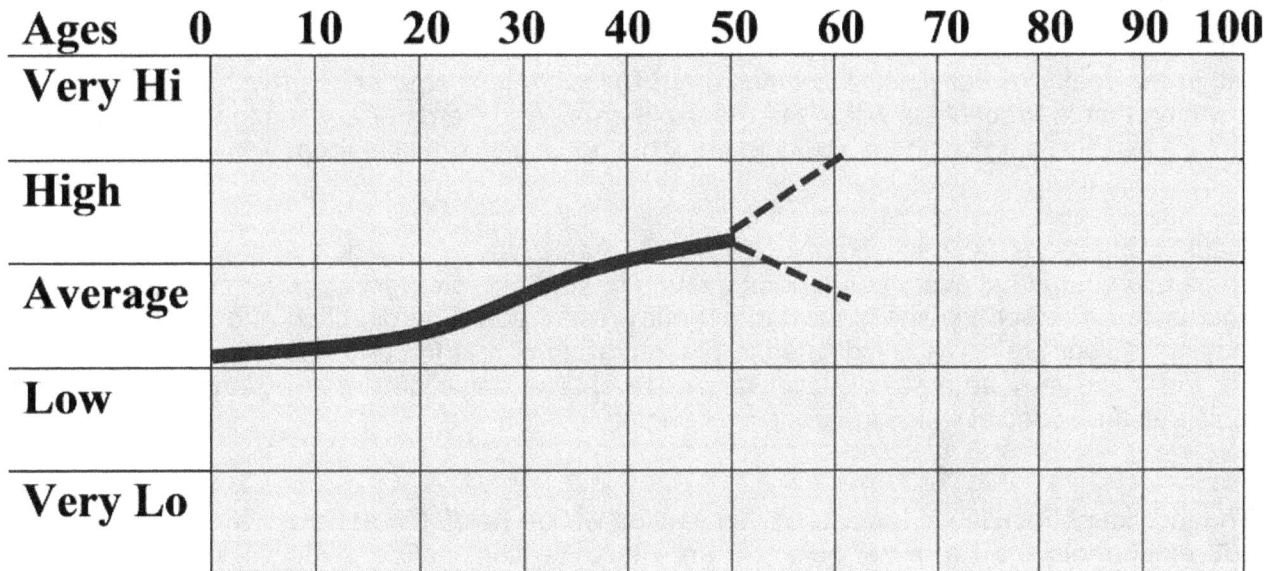

Ages	0	10	20	30	40	50	60	70	80	90	100
Very Hi											
High											
Average											
Low											
Very Lo											

Finally, make a second line from the present through the next ten-year period, as shown above, but representing the lowest plausible quality for the next life stage. This is your pessimistic projection for this domain..

Keep in mind that these projections are estimations. Also, keep in mind that these projections should be within the limits of plausibility. How do we define plausibility?

One way is shown in the Plausible area in the diagram below. The area outside the cone formed by your two projections is represented in the Possible area.

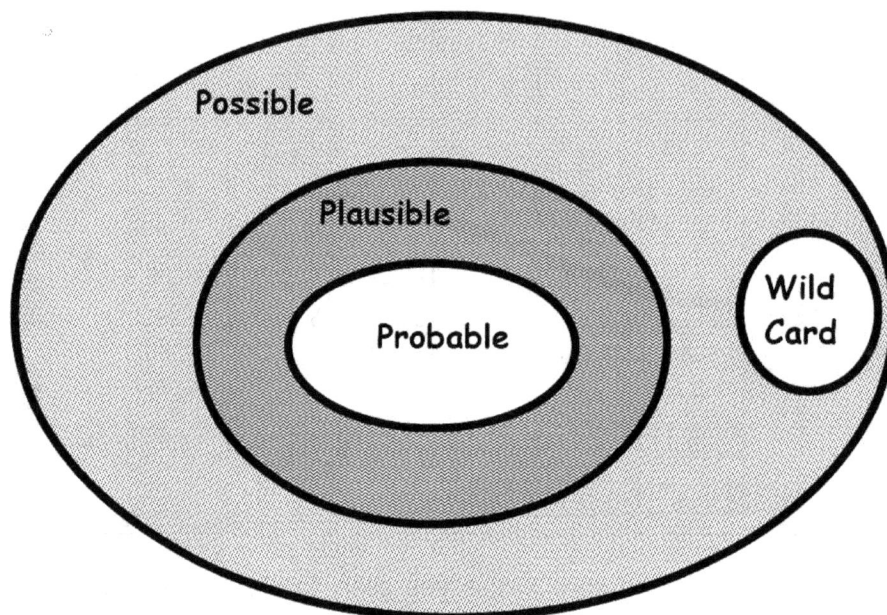

This diagram illustrates the possibilities that exist in the future, and shows that *everything* is within the realm of Possible, (the outer ring). Plausible is a smaller area within Possible, and anything that is Probable is within the Plausible area. Wild Cards (like winning the lottery, being hit by a meteor, etc.) are in the possible area, but not in the plausible area.

Blank workspaces for each domain follow. On each, you will mark the quality level of that domain in your life at every ten-year interval up to your present age. Look for changes in levels and for the direction the line is moving at your present age. The direction and angle of the line leading to your present age indicate the present trend of that force in your life. The direction of the trend line may be upward, downward or level. The angle of that direction from horizontal indicates the speed at which the trend is changing.

The individual domain worksheets in this section will be helpful in several ways. The lines that you extend into the future will help you (in a later section) define plausible scenarios for the future. The completed worksheets will help you create a framework of information that will become the basis for your scenarios about the future.

Activities

The Activities domain includes school, training, self-improvement, work or career, religion, sports, hobbies, travel, and the all other things you do. Some activities, such as addictions, are negative or destructive, and can also become driving forces.

Activities Domain

Ages	0	10	20	30	40	50	60	70	80	90	100
Very Hi											
High											
Average											
Low											
Very Lo											

To create a graph
1- Determine the quality levels of the *activities* in your life during each of the ten-year periods up to your present age. Draw a line across each period (the line can slope up, down, stay level or have changes), stopping at your present age. This line represents your opinion of the quality of the *activities* in your life from birth to the present. Note the direction (up, down, level) at the present. This indicates the direction of the current trend of your satisfaction with the *activities* in your life.
2- Starting at your present age, draw a line that represents the best plausible or optimistic projection of your *activities* through the next life stage or ten years.
3- Starting at your present age, draw a line that represents the worst plausible or pessimistic projection of your *activities* through the next life stage or ten years.

What is your present level of satisfaction with your *activities*?

What would you like to change?

What would you have to do to initiate a change?

Finances

The finances domain includes everything that has to do with your finances, including your income, expenses, assets, liabilities, investments, insurance, taxes, credit cards, and all the time you spend thinking (or worrying) about your financial responsibilities or opportunities.

Finances Domain

Ages	0	10	20	30	40	50	60	70	80	90	100
Very Hi											
High											
Average											
Low											
Very Lo											

To create a graph

1- Determine the quality levels of the *finances* in your life during each of the ten-year periods up to your present age. Draw a line across each period (the line can slope up, down, stay level or have changes), stopping at your present age. This line represents your opinion of the quality of the *finances* in your life from birth to the present. Note the direction (up, down, level) at the present. This indicates the direction of the current trend of your satisfaction with the *finances* in your life.

2- Starting at your present age, draw a line that represents the best plausible or optimistic projection of your *finances* through the next life stage or ten years.

3- Starting at your present age, draw a line that represents the worst plausible or pessimistic projection of your *finances* through the next life stage or ten years.

What is your present level of satisfaction with your *finances?*

What would you like to change?

What would you have to do to initiate a change?

Health

The health domain includes everything related to your physical, emotional and mental health. This includes your health status, conditions or diseases, medications, diet and exercise, medical care, and personal care that you receive.

Health Domain

Ages	0	10	20	30	40	50	60	70	80	90	100
Very Hi											
High											
Average											
Low											
Very Lo											

To create a graph

1- Determine the quality levels of the *health domain* in your life during each of the ten-year periods up to your present age. Draw a line across each period (the line can slope up, down, stay level or have changes), stopping at your present age. This line represents your opinion of the quality of the *health domain* in your life from birth to the present. Note the direction (up, down, level) at the present. This indicates the direction of the current trend of your satisfaction with the *health domain* in your life.

2- Starting at your present age, draw a line that represents the best plausible or optimistic projection of your *health* through the next life stage or ten years.

3- Starting at your present age, draw a line that represents the worst plausible or pessimistic projection of your *health* through the next life stage or ten years.

What is your present level of satisfaction with your *health*?

What would you like to change?

What would you have to do to initiate a change?

Housing

The housing domain includes your home, the neighborhood and community you live in, your country (including its political and economic systems), and the climate for your region of the world. If you live in (or expect to live in) a care facility, that is also part of your housing domain.

Housing Domain

Ages	0	10	20	30	40	50	60	70	80	90	100
Very Hi											
High											
Average											
Low											
Very Lo											

To create a graph

1- Determine the quality levels of the *housing domain* in your life during each of the ten-year periods up to your present age. Draw a line across each period (the line can slope up, down, stay level or have changes), stopping at your present age. This line represents your opinion of the quality of the *housing domain* in your life from birth to the present. Note the direction (up, down, level) at the present. This indicates the direction of the current trend of your satisfaction with the *housing domain* in your life. Remember that this domain includes all aspects of housing, from your home and community to world region and climate.

2- Starting at your present age, draw a line that represents the best plausible or optimistic projection of your *housing* through the next life stage or ten years.

3- Starting at your present age, draw a line that represents the worst plausible or pessimistic projection of your *housing* through the next life stage or ten years.

What is your present level of satisfaction with your *housing*?

What would you like to change?

What would you have to do to initiate a change?

Social

The Social domain starts with family and closest friends, then expands outward to embrace your friends, co-workers, advisors, and community. Sociology and other disciplines often use an illustration of nested circles to demonstrate some of these social relationships.

Social Domain

Ages	0	10	20	30	40	50	60	70	80	90	100
Very Hi											
High											
Average											
Low											
Very Lo											

To create a graph

1- Determine the quality levels of the *social domain* in your life during each of the ten-year periods up to your present age. Draw a line across each period (the line can slope up, down, stay level or have changes), stopping at your present age. This line represents your opinion of the quality of the *social domain* in your life from birth to the present. Note the direction (up, down, level) at the present. This indicates the direction of the current trend of your satisfaction with the *social domain* in your life.

2- Starting at your present age, draw a line that represents the best plausible or most optimistic projection of your *social life* through the next life stage or ten years.

3- Starting at your present age, draw a line that represents the worst plausible or pessimistic projection of your *social life* through the next life stage or ten years.

What is your present level of satisfaction with your *social domain*?

What would you like to change?

What would you have to do to initiate a change?

Transportation

The Transportation domain includes all forms of mobility, including walking, bicycles, wheelchairs, cars, taxis, buses, boats, airplanes and any other form of transportation.

Transportation Domain

Ages	0	10	20	30	40	50	60	70	80	90	100
Very Hi											
High											
Average											
Low											
Very Lo											

To create a graph

1- Determine the quality levels of the *transportation domain* in your life during each of the ten-year periods up to your present age. Draw a line across each period (the line can slope up, down, stay level or have changes), stopping at your present age. This line represents your opinion of the quality of this domain in your life from birth to the present. Note the direction (up, down, level) at the present. This indicates the direction of the current trend of your satisfaction with this domain in your life.

2- Starting at your present age, draw a line that represents the best plausible or optimistic projection of this domain through the next life stage or ten years.

3- Starting at your present age, draw a line that represents the worst plausible or pessimistic projection of your *transportation* through the next life stage or ten years.

What is your present level of satisfaction with your *transportation?*

What would you like to change?

What would you have to do to initiate a change?

Driving forces in your life

During *each* stage of your life, one or two domains will probably dominate the important changes in your life. The table below shows some of the common driving forces in each stage of life. These are simply indicators, a starting point.

Common driving forces for each life stage

Life Stage	Driving force 1	Driving force 2
Infant	Social- family	Activities- learning
Child	Social- family	Activities- school
Adolescent	Social- peers; independence	Activities- school, sports
Young adult	Activities- School, career	Social
Adult	Social- family	Activities- career
Middle age	Activities- career	Social- family Health
Independent elder	Activities- retirement	Health
Vulnerable elder	Health- declining	Social – family or Housing- care facility
Dependent elder	Health- declining	Social – family or Housing- care facility
End of life	Health- terminal	Social – family or Housing – care facility

.As you look forward to the coming life stage, which domains or forces are likely to be dominant in your future. Which forces will bring about change in your life? List the two (or three) domains or forces that you believe will be dominant in your next life stage.

Dominant force (domain) #1	
Dominant force (domain) #2	
Dominant force (domain) #3	

Scanning your environment and STEEP

Awareness of changes in your community and the national economy as well as changing social or technological trends in the world around you should be built into your strategies and action plans. This can translate into simple awareness —for example, in your community, be aware of planned future projects that might affect your family or your property, positively or negatively. Also, be aware of movements or activity to create laws or regulations that may impact you.

Many futurists use the mnemonic "STEEP" to remind them of some of the outside forces that may affect our lives.

Social forces

Technological forces

Economic forces

Ecologic forces

Political forces

Which of these forces are likely to have a strong impact on your life over the next ten years?

In the worksheet on the next page, consider these forces and how each one could affect you at a local, national, or international level.

STEEP Scanning Worksheet

	World	National	Local
Social			
Technology			
Economic			
Ecologic			
Political			

Life Events
(Chapter 7 in It's YOUR Future…)

Life events are simply the things that happen in our lives. Some events are more important than others, and some events (turning point events, for example) may actually change the direction of your life. Marriage, divorce, birth of a child, and retirement are all examples of turning point events. Other events such as birthdays and anniversaries may simply be milestones, with little or no impact. As you look ahead for events in your future, your concerns will lie with probabilities and impacts.

If an event has no impact, regardless of probability, it does not require much preparation. Events that have a high probability of occurrence and a high impact are events that you will want to prepare and plan for. Events with a low probability of occurrence, but a high impact are called wild cards, for which you may want to make contingency plans.

	Considerations for Personal Futures	Examples
When	When is the event likely to occur?	At what age or life stage?
Type	What type of event is this? Turning point Life cycle/biologic Legal Intentional/choice Unintentional Other	Marriage, children, divorce Growth, puberty, menopause Voting age, retirement age Marriage, children, divorce Deaths of family or friends Accident, job loss, anniversaries
Impact	What is the impact of the event?	What is the severity? Physical, emotional, financial?
Probability	What is the probability of this event occurring?	During your life? During any particular time period?
Domain	Within which domain does an event occur? Activities Finances Health Housing Social Transportation	Complete education, start career Save or invest for retirement Exercise to maintain health Move to a different home Birth of a child Learn to drive a car

Reading the table on the previous page, it is apparent we can look at *some* events as foreknowns. We can be pretty certain they will happen.

Based on the experiences of others who have already experienced these events, it is possible to anticipate, at least to some degree, the timing, probability, and impacts of many events. When compared with life stages and personal domains, this gives us a third perspective of the future. Later, we will combine these three perspectives (stages, domains, and events) into a framework that summarizes your knowledge of your futures.

Events that commonly occur during specific life stages

On the next page is a table of common events in life and the life stages in which those events are likely to occur. This listing is intended to give you some indication of events to anticipate or prepare for at different times of life. For the most part, these events are common in the United States middle class, but not common everywhere. Some events, marriage and first births for example, are affected by cultural patterns and socio-economic status.

Examples of common life events

Life Stage	Common Events	High impact Events
Infant	Learning, walk, talk Minor illnesses	Serious illness
Child	School Growth Minor injuries and illnesses	Serious illness Bullying Parents divorce
Adolescent	Complete required schooling Puberty, emotions, sex Physical growth Begin driving Risky behaviors	Accidents, serious injuries Arrest Pregnancy Parents divorce Death of parent or friend
Young adult	Complete higher education Begin career Move to own housing Marriage First child	Accidents Illness or injury of child Job loss
Adult	Career pressures- advances Managing family Last child	Financial pressures Divorce Job loss
Middle age	Menopause-end child bearing Aging signs Empty nest Grandchildren Parents retire Peak earnings, savings	Serious or chronic illness, self or spouse. Parent illness or death Crime victim Job loss Divorce
Independent elder	Eligible for retirement Social Security, Medicare (U.S.) Work/retirement choices Discretionary time Great grandchildren Increased aging signs Relocate, new friends Travel Problems in children's lives	Retirement Changing roles & social Serious illness, self or spouse Death of spouse Become caregiver Stop driving
Vulnerable elder	Frailty Cognitive problems Risk of falls Risk of scams, victim of crime	Falls, injuries Assisted living
Dependent elder	Reduced activities Increased medical Reduced social	Dependent on others Losing control of life Nursing home
End of life	Reduced activities and social Increased medical Good-byes	Terminal diagnosis Hospice

Life Events Worksheet

Use the following worksheet to list events that you anticipate in your life during the life stage for which you are going to plan. Use the forces listed in the Domains column as reminders for events.

Domains and Sub-forces	High probability, high impact events in your life (for strategic planning)	High impact-child, parent, other	Wild card events
Activities School, training Career, work Sports, hobbies Religion			
Finances Income, investments Expenses, debt			
Health Condition Medication Care			
Housing Home Community Country, region			
Social Family Friends Community			
Transportation Mobility Personal, auto Public			

Example: Life Events Worksheet - Young Adult stage

Domain Sub-forces	High probability, high impact events	High impact- child, parent, other	Wild card events
Activities School, training Career, work Sports, hobbies Religion	Finish schooling Start career Promotion	Parents middle age, many changes Children infants	Promoted! Fired!
Finances Income, investments Expenses, debt	Earning own income, End parents support. Finance car/house Excessive debt	Parents don't help Two incomes	Major Bonus Major loss
Health Condition Medication Care	Expecting! Injury or major illness	Grandparent/parent illness	Serious illness Crime victim
Housing Home Community Country, region	Moving First apartment First home	We/Parents move away	Transferred to New York! Transferred overseas
Social Family Friends Community	Marriage First child Marital problems Job/family conflicts	Parents divorce Wife starts work Risk-grandparent health	Twins!
Transportation Mobility Personal, auto Public	Used car, high maintenance Traffic tickets First new car Auto accident	Family injured	Home office Very long commute

Personal Values Worksheet
(Chapter 8 in It's YOUR Future…)

Values- what is important to you? This worksheet asks you to compare and rank your values. In the Rank column, select the value that is most important to you and enter the number 1. Then pick the second, third and on to the end of your list. For future reference, list your values in numerical order in the last column.

Value	Rank	List your Values in order of importance to you	Rank
Career			1
Professional relationships			2
Recognition			3
Power or influence			4
Income			5
Financial security			6
Net worth			7
Family			8
Family activities			9
Personal/family image			10
Ethics/principles			11
Religion			12
Independence			13
Contribution to others			14
Challenge/risk			15
Geographic location			16
Health			17
Honesty			18
Truthfulness			19
			20
			21
			22
			23
			24
			25
			26
			27
			28
			29
			30

Example: Values worksheet for Young Adult

Value	Rank	List your Values in order of importance to you	
Career	3	family	1
Professional relationships		friends	2
Recognition	5	education/career	3
Power or influence	9	income	4
Income	4	recognition	5
Financial security		Personal image	6
Net worth	8	Location-New York!	7
Family	1	Net worth	8
Family activities		influence	9
Personal/family image	6	ethics	10
Ethics/principles	10	independence	11
Religion			12
Independence	11		13
Contribution to others			14
Challenge/risk			15
Geographic location	7		16
Education	3		17
Friends	2		18

Example: Values Worksheet for Young adult

Example: Values Worksheet for Independent Elder

Value	Rank	List your Values in order of importance to you	Rank
Career		Spouse and family	1
Professional relationships		Health	2
Recognition		Independence	3
Power or influence		Financial security	4
Income	5	Income	5
Financial security	4	Geographic location- warm!	6
Net worth		Ethics and principles	7
Family	1	Family activities	8
Family activities	8	Contribution to others	9
Personal/family image			10
Ethics/principles	7		11
Religion			12
Independence	3		13
Contribution to others	9		14
Challenge/risk			15
Geographic location	6		16
Health	2		17

Compare these two examples and note how values may change from one life stage to another.

Strengths, Weaknesses, Opportunities, and Threats
(Chapter 9 in It's YOUR Future…)

This technique is usually referred to as "SWOT" and starts with a simple self analysis of your personal strengths and weaknesses. This is an internal analysis.

SWOT Worksheets

Strengths and Weaknesses

Internal	Strengths (Knowledge, abilities, skills, experience)	Weaknesses (Knowledge, abilities, skills, experience)
Activities		
Finance		
Health		
Housing		
Social		
Transport (Mobility)		

An example of a completed Strengths and Weaknesses worksheet

Internal Factors	My Strengths (Knowledge, abilities, skills, experience)	My Weaknesses (Knowledge, abilities, skills, experience)
Activities (School, career, sports, religion)	Good education, training, experience. Athletic. Write, speak, computer	Math skills. Artistic. English only
Finance	Good income. Good credit history. Adequate insurance	Big mortgage. Credit card debt. High taxes. Inadequate retirement fund
Health	Excellent health. Good physical condition	Getting older. Family history of cancer
Housing	Good home. Good neighborhood	Big mortgage. High maintenance
Social	Close, supportive family. Good appearance, social skills. Very good references	Not good networker. Not socially aggressive
Transport (Mobility)	Two reliable cars. Short commute	Inadequate public transport. Fear of flying

The Opportunities and Threats worksheet offers an external analysis of what you recognize as opportunities or threats that exist in the world around you.

Opportunities

External Opportunities	Global	National	Local
Social			
Technology			
Economy			
Ecology			
Politics			

Threats

External Threats	Global	National	Local
Social			
Technology			
Economy			
Ecology			
Politics			

Examples of the completed Opportunities and Threats worksheets.

External Opportunities	Global	National	Local
Social	Improving healthcare worldwide. Slowing population growth	Rising employment	Community involvement
Technology	Easy communication Availability of knowledge Increasing availability of solar and wind power	Nanotech/medical Stem cell medicine Preventive medicine	Home power (solar, wind) generation Preventive medicine
Economy	International growth in markets Greater global interdependence	Economic growth Increasing employment	Home value rising Investment opportunities
Ecology	Awareness of ecological balance	Efforts to reduce impacts on planet	Improved water and drainage systems
Politics	Reduction of conflicts	Increasing transparency Increasing access to info	Increasing awareness of public and voters

External Threats	Global	National	Local
Social	Wars Hunger, underemployment	Flu Drugs and addiction	Immigration Gang problems Unemployment
Technology	Nuclear weapons Space weapons	Pollution	New technology is changing skill requirements at work
Economy	Recession Protectionism Resource shortages	Higher taxes Inflation Recession	Higher taxes Unemployment
Ecology	Warming Water shortages	Combat warming Continued reliance on coal and oil	Hurricanes Earthquakes Flooding
Politics	Hot war Trade war	Excessive regulation Inadequate regulation	Zoning Streets Development

The Futures Wheel
(Chapter 9 in It's YOUR Future...)

The futures wheel is a tool that is used by most futurists. It is also called a mind map, and can be very simple, like the example below. Futures Wheels can become complex as more levels are added. The futures wheel is very effective for brainstorming, whether you are working alone or in a group. You can draw one anywhere, on paper, on a whiteboard or in your computer.
The idea is to start with a simple question or problem, then branch out from that idea to directly related ideas, effect, impacts or whatever you are looking for.

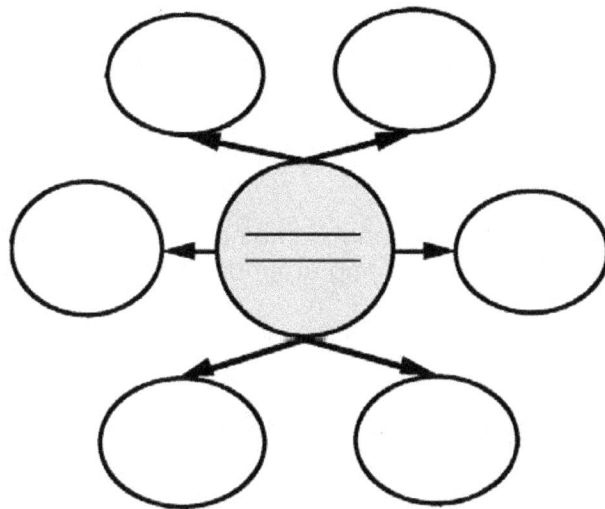

A basic futures wheel showing spaces for the first level of impacts.

Here is an example of personal futures wheel, starting with your original idea then expanding to your six personal domains.

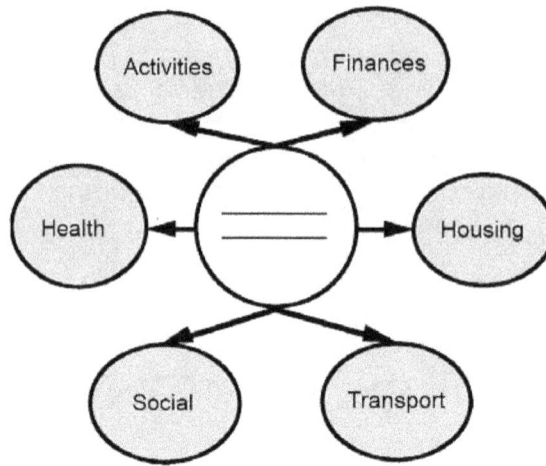

A personal futures wheel with the six personal domains shown at the first level.
From each of the direct impacts in the first ring around your main question or idea, branch again to secondary ideas or impacts.

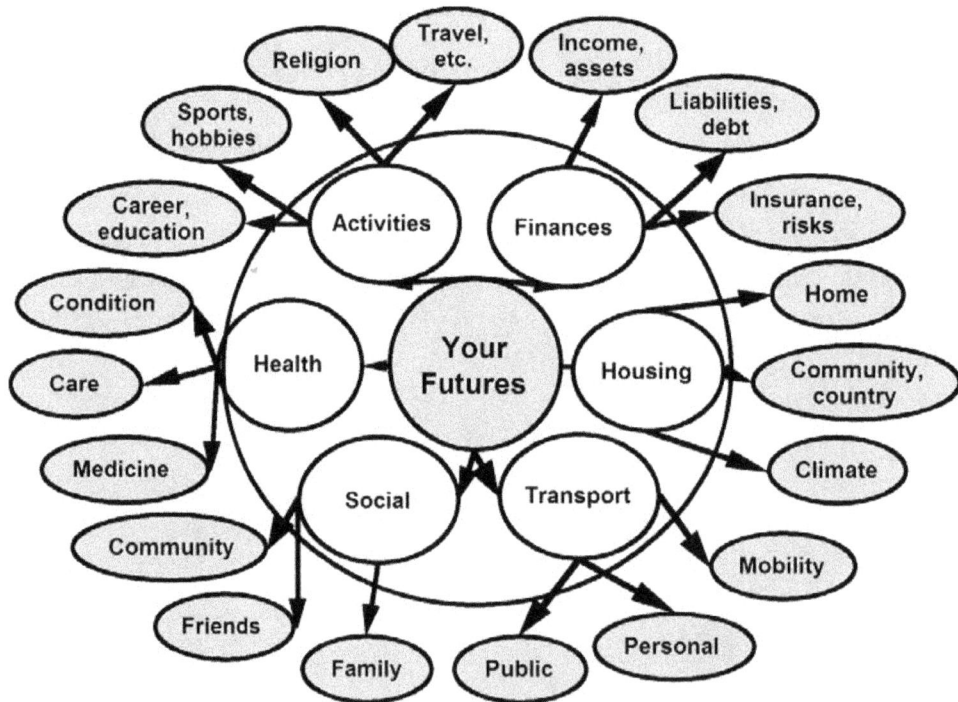

A personal futures wheel expanded to the second level of impacts.

Next, branch again to a third ring of impacts. When you are drawing on paper or a whiteboard, futures wheels start getting messy at this level, but they still work!

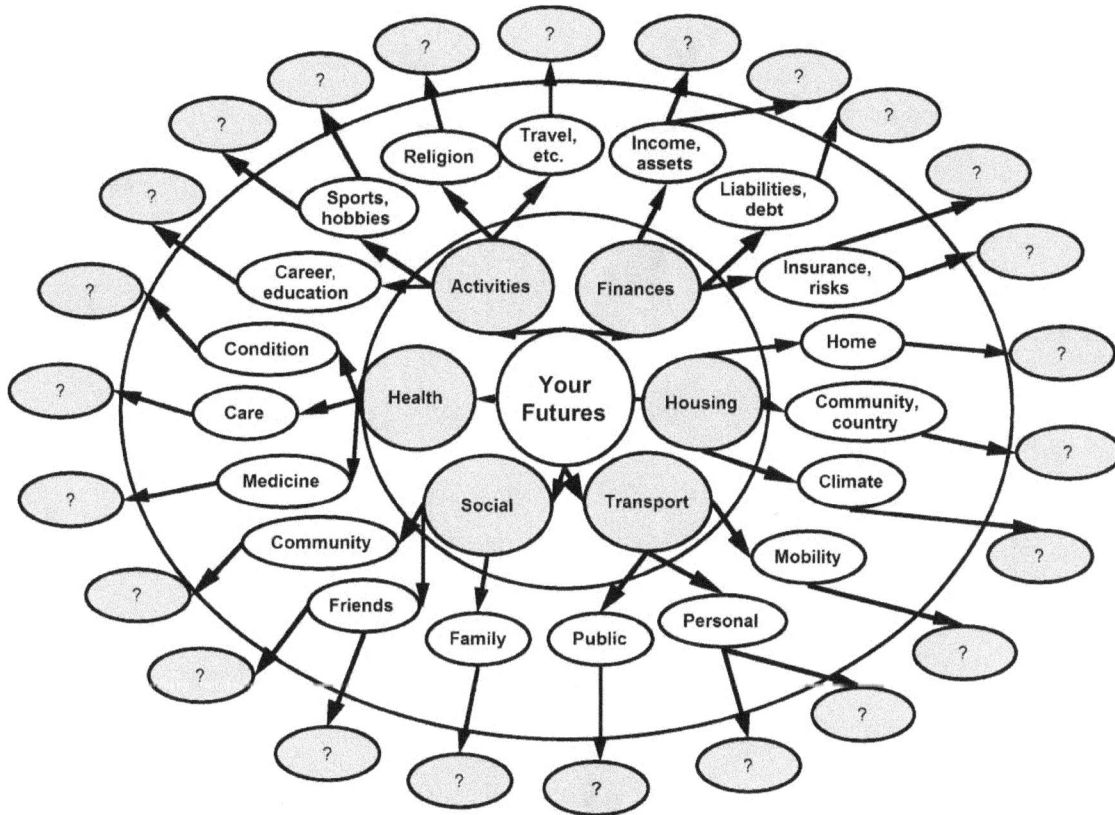

A personal futures wheel expanded to the third ring of impacts.

The futures wheel is very versatile. You will find it helpful in sorting out ideas or simply thinking about the future or other concepts. If you have occasion to speak to a group at school or at work, the futures wheel is a great tool for brainstorming and collecting ideas or information. All you need is a blank space and something you can write with.

Section II - Explore Your Futures with Scenarios

(Chapters 10,11,12,13 in It's YOUR Future...)

Worksheets for five scenarios

Using information from the worksheets that you have already created, fill in the scenario worksheets on the next pages with events that fit within each scenario column.

The Continuation of the Present scenario is based on your estimate of the probable future if there is no major change and you take no action to create change.

Refer back to the graphs you created in the Personal Domains section and the two lines you extended into the future for each graph. The top lines for each domain are the basis for the Best Plausible scenario. The lower lines make up the Worst Plausible scenario.

The Wild Card scenario includes events that are possible, but not probable as you see your future at this time.

Also from the chapter on personal domains, recall the two domains (driving forces) that you expected to be dominant in bringing about change in your life during this stage. As you fill in the worksheet, think about how events may vary in those two domains in each of the scenarios you are building.

For example, if a dominant domain during this stage of your life is the Activities Domain, and specifically your career, how might your career vary between the positive scenario and the negative scenario? In the positive scenario you may have great successes in your career, while in your negative scenario you may struggle or even lose your job.

If you have goals or plans that you are already working on, do they affect these scenarios? Do your values have any impact?

Continuation of the Present scenario

Forces and factors	Anticipated high impact, high probability events
Activities	
Finances	
Health	
Housing	
Social	
Transportation	
Goals, plans, values	

Best Plausible scenario

Forces and factors	Anticipated high impact, high probability events plus impacts of positive forces
Activities	
Finances	
Health	
Housing	
Social	
Transportation	
Goals, plans, values	

Aspirational scenario

Forces and factors	Anticipated high impact, high probability events plus effects of motivated, intentional change
Activities	
Finances	
Health	
Housing	
Social	
Transportation	
Goals, plans, values	

Wild Card scenario

Forces and factors	Anticipated high impact, high probability events plus one or more low-probability , high-impact events
Activities	
Finances	
Health	
Housing	
Social	
Transportation	
Goals, plans, values	

Worst Plausible scenario

Forces and factors	Anticipated high impact, high probability events plus impacts of negative forces
Activities	
Finances	
Health	
Housing	
Social	
Transportation	
Goals, plans, values	

Example: Four Scenario Worksheets for the Young Adult stage

Forces and factors	Continuation of the present scenario	Best plausible scenario	Wild Card Scenario *(Negative)*	Worst Plausible Scenario
Activities	Graduate-good grades and recommendations Start a good job	Graduate with MS, honors and recommendation Recruited into excellent career position	Unable to find a good job-working as low level temp	Graduated but no honors or recommendation Temp work
Finances	Medium income, good benefits Low debt-have savings and reserve	Good income, Good savings, no debt No financial problems!	Low income, no savings, can't afford to do anything! No credit. No health insurance Barely paying college loans	Low starting pay, No benefits Too much debt
Health	Good health	Great health-working out- good checkup	Too tired to work out	Risky work environment
Housing	Own apartment in home city	Relocated to new York. Have apartment	Living with parents	Apartment OK - nothing special. Still in home town
Social	Close with parents and family Marriage to friend from HS and college Two children- everyone's healthy	Meeting lots of new people. Met Miss Right - marriage at 27 First child— grandparents all happy! Planning another.	Living with parents. Not much social life, can't afford to date	Family is encouraging. Still see old friends
Transportation	Van for family, older sports car for me	Company car and good public transport	Old car	Public transit
Goals, plans & values	Start own business within 10 years Get GOOD education for kids-spend time with them!	Position myself in the company to climb gradually—keep time to spend with family. Start planning house or larger flat	Get a good job, get on career track	Climb the ladder by working hard and smart Avoid debt—Look for good mate

Scenario Narratives-
(Chapter 13 in It's YOUR Future...)

From the information you have placed in each scenario column of the worksheet, write a story about your life during the next ten years or your next life stage. Spend some time and use your imagination to make each story fit together in a logical manner. Keep in mind that what you are doing in this workbook is making educated guesses about the future. By creating narratives you are developing an understanding of what must happen to make the elements in your scenario work together

In future years, you will see signals that will indicate which scenarios will or will not come about. That should give you time to adjust and prepare to deal with those changes.

Scenario I – Continuation of the present

Scenario Example

It's late Spring in New York City and the weather is much like the week when I graduated six years ago...beautiful. My wife has planned a birthday party for my 3 year old daughter and me (she was born two days after my 27th birthday). Just the four of us (two year old son) for Pizza in the park.

The past ten years have been incredible! When I graduated, with my Master's degree, I was really on track, I had the degree, the references, even a great internship. But the economy was in the tank, and there just weren't any jobs in my field. After sending out resumes for months, I was really discouraged. Then the phone call from a small company in New York that I'd never heard of. We talked for an hour on the phone, then they promised to call back. And they invited me to New York for an interview and sent me a ticket. The pay wasn't great, but the opportunity was, and I accepted their offer.

I went home to pack, called my girl friend and asked her to marry me and go to New York and she said yes! We found a flat near Central Park and I went to work. And work is what I did. It was a real learning experience. New York City is an expensive place to live, even with two incomes, but we both loved living here. I got some small promotions, and we're actually saving money. College loans are paid off and we're thinking about buying a home, but for the moment we're better off renting. We don't own a car because it's more practical, and cheaper, to use cabs and public transportation.

Turning thirty reminds me, it's time to make a new plan for the nest stage of our life—all four of us!

Section III- Create Your Future—The Future You Want to Live

(Chapter 14, 15, 16 17 in *It's YOUR Future...*)

A strategic plan is just what the name implies- a plan for your future based on strategies to achieve a future that you have envisioned.

This implies that in order to strategize and plan, you must first determine what future you want. If you think about the future you would like to have during your next ten years of your life, what future do you see, or envision? That will be the <u>first step</u> in your strategic plan, creating a vision of the future—your destination in the future.

<u>Next</u>, you will consider the high impact events that are likely to happen during the time period for which you are planning. Do you have a mission for this period of life? Something critical that must be achieved? Do you have goals or desires that that you have not included in your vision? Now is the time to write all the things down in one place and get ready to plan to achieve or deal with your Interests and concerns over this stage of your life.

The <u>third step</u> in your strategic planning process is to create strategies that will help you achieve your goals and your vision of the future as well as deal with anticipated high impact events that may occur.

<u>Fourth</u>, you will develop an action plan— actions you will take each year, in sequence.

<u>Fifth</u> you will devise contingency plans to deal with the wild cards that may occur during this life stage. These are high impact events that are unlikely to occur, but if they do, you will have a contingency plan in place.

The <u>final step</u> is to live the plan you have created. Take the actions and follow the strategies you have selected to achieve your future, but continue to monitor your plan, your life, and the world around you. Has anything changed that affects your plan? If so, then adjust your plan to fit the new circumstances. Your strategic plan is simply a tool that you can use. Use it to help you achieve the future you prefer.

Your vision of your future

Think of one sentence that describes your image of how you would like your life to be in the future. The emphasis here is on your desired or preferred future.

A vision of the future may mean many things. For organizations conducting strategic planning, a vision is an image of the organization at some time in the future, usually ten to twenty years away. When you looked at the stages of life, you built mental images of the various stages, then set out to understand the next stage in your life. So now, when you are presented with the need to create a vision of the future, is that for the next stage of life, or for all of life? One answer is, both.

At this point in your planning, you should be able to describe a clear vision for the next stage of your life, but what about the whole of life? One area you have not dealt with yet in your preparations is emotion. What will make you happy in and with your life? What will give you contentment? Satisfaction? A feeling of accomplishment? Use the worksheet below to collect some thoughts about your vision of the future.

Worksheet	Your vision for each domain for this stage
Activities What do you want to do? Career? Travel? Sport? Religion?	
Finances What's important financially? Income? Net worth? Insurance? Estate?	
Health How do you see your health? What care will you need?	
Housing Where will you live?	
Social Who will be close to you? What groups will be important?	
Transportation What will be your means of transport?	

Now, ask yourself: about your values. What or who is really important in your life? Family? Career? Wealth? Ethics? Knowledge?

What do you want to achieve during this life stage? Career advancement? Raise family? Educate your children? Travel? Accumulate? Change the world?

Summarize all of this into one sentence about your preferred future. Two at the most. This written vision should give you direction, declare where you are going, what you want to achieve and, by implication, what you want to avoid.

To create your vision for the next stage of your life, start with a mental image of where you want your life to be at the end of your next life stage. Consider each of your domains, then bring them together in one image.

Write in one or two memorable sentences your vision of where you want your life to be at the end of your next life stage.

```



```

Let's take this one more step. What do you want in your future for the rest of your life, beyond the next life stage? Do you want a long life? A healthy life? A close family throughout life? What will be important in retirement? At the end of your life?

```



```

Example of a personal vision for the future:
Have a close, loving family enjoying a healthy, upper-middleclass life that keeps me involved and busy with family, business and community for the rest of my life. Live healthy beyond 100! When my life ends, that event should be free of pain, sorrow or difficulties for my family.

Strategies to Achieve Your Vision
(Chapter 16 in It's YOUR Future...)

For your vision of your future, develop strategies to *achieve* that vision. Review your scenarios and devise strategies to deal with futures that may occur.

For the negative or worst plausible scenario where everything goes wrong, devise strategies to *prevent, avoid or deal with* that future. Think in terms of "If...then" strategies. "If this happens, then my strategy becomes..."

A strategy is a general approach or technique for achieving or dealing with a situation. A more detailed plan for achieving your strategy will come later in your Action Plan. For example, if you are in a difficult career situation, you might change employers, or even change careers. To change careers, you may have to return to school for new training and new credentials.

Strategies to improve or maintain your health for the long term might include changes in your diet, an increase in exercise, stop smoking or other behavioral changes. Housing strategies may include downsizing when the children leave, or a move to a different climate.

Within each strategy, you may later set goals that relate to executing the strategy, and tasks that much be accomplished to reach each goal.

.

Strategies for your future

A strategy is simply one way to do something. Chess is a game of strategies in which the player with the best strategies will probably win. You are looking for strategies to achieve your vision of the future and to deal with probable future events, so spend some time thinking about how to devise the best strategies to achieve your vision.

Domains	Strategies to achieve goals, mission and vision	Strategies to avoid or reduce impacts of probable events
Activities		
Finances		
Health		
Housing		
Social		
Transportation		

Consider your strategies for each domain, particularly for events that are high impact events that have a high probability of occurrence. You will also (on another worksheet) develop contingency plans for high impact events with a low probability of occurrence.

Example: Strategies for the future worksheet- Young adult

Domains	Strategies to achieve goals, mission and vision	Strategies to avoid or reduce impacts of probable events
Activities	Maximize GPA, honors, achievements and recommendations. Get documents. Target top intern positions Study prospective employers-find best	Pace myself- think 40+ year career- don't burnout. Don't over commit
Finances	Minimize college debt Protect credit rating Start saving Maximize income Get health insurance	Budget to reduce school debt avoid new debt Avoid credit card debt!
Health	Maintain health at highest possible level Avoid injury or illness	Avoid risky habits
Housing	Identify employers that need me in NYC Research best housing options for family	Avoid risky neighborhoods, communities or countries
Social	Keep family close Marry someone who will be a partner Good schools for kids	Don't get over involved in community Don't social climb
Transportation	Safe reliable and affordable Short commutes to work and schools	Buy cars to drive 10 years

Action Plans for Your Future
(Chapter 17 in It's YOUR Future...)

Now you must turn your strategies into actions. What actions must you take, starting today, to achieve your preferred future? What is the best sequence for those actions?

These are the actions that can change your future. Until you actually take action, nothing in your planning will change your future.

This is the central document of your strategic plan. You can (and should) modify or change your plan as you go along, because events in your life will not unfold according to plan, so stay flexible, but keep working toward your preferred future.

Year	Actions to be taken Activities-Finances-Health-Housing-Social -Transportation
2013	
2014	
2015	
2016	
2017	
2018	
2019	
2020	
2021	
2022	
2023	
2024	

Example: Action Plan Worksheet

Year	Actions to be taken Activities-Finances-Health-Housing-Social -Transportation
2011	Age 20-Complete major pre-requisites *Start Jr year at university*
2012	21-Complete Jr year Start Sr year
2013	22-Graduate Apply for Masters—take exam—apply for fellowship Start Masters--network Company research-apply for internship
2014	23-Internship Job research Write resume, get letters of recommendation
2015	24-Submit resume's Interviews Attend job fairs Network Get hired! Graduate Master's program! Get an apartment
2016	25- Move to NYC! Find Miss Right
2017	26-Focus on establishing solid career Start retirement saving Save for home—manage credit record
2018	27- Family starting?- check neighborhoods and schools
2019	28-Finish paying off college loans—increase savings and investments No short term debt Evaluate business cycle/real estate/investment climate
2020	29-Evaluate career status-seek international experience Stay at this job or look elsewhere? Explore owning home-prepare Evaluate-working from home
2021	30-Physical checkup Grampa turns 80—keep relationship close Start planning for next stage of life

Backcasting

The Backcasting worksheet is simply a tool for working backwards from the future. Imagine yourself in the life you are planning to achieve, but ten years from now. You have achieved your vision! What was the *last* action you had to take? And the one before that?

This will be helpful in developing the sequence of actions you must take to achieve your vision of your future.

Year	Actions to be taken Activities-Finances-Health-Housing-Social -Transportation
2024	
2023	
2022	
2021	
2020	
2019	
2018	
2017	
2016	
2015	
2014	
2013	

Analyzing Your Plan
(Chapter 18 in It's YOUR Future...)

Once you have completed your action plan, you should analyze it to see if there is anything you have overlooked. Two worksheets follow, Vulnerability Analysis and Gap Analysis.

Vulnerability Analysis

First is the vulnerability analysis. Ask yourself which event or events could occur that would cause things to fall apart in your life. Losing a job or a serious health problem might do it, but so might a fire, hurricane or earthquake.

The idea here is to see what kind of event it would take to shatter your life, then consider ways to prevent those events or reduce their impacts. Keep in mind the potential for cascading events, where one event triggers another, which triggers another. (For example; due to poor health, lost job, which terminated health insurance, etc.).

	Vulnerabilities	Risk reduction
Activities		
Finances		
Health		
Housing		
Social		
Transportation		

Example: Vulnerability Analysis for a Young Adult.

	Vulnerabilities	Risk reduction
Activities	Loss of spouse's job Writing career fails to develop	Increase my income Teach or full-time work
Finances	Loss of income and insurance	Second income and Savings Alternate insurance
Health	Serious illness or injury, self or spouse	Insurance Good health, physical condition
Housing	Earthquake, tsunami Wildfires Over-mortgaged	Home not near waterfront Home not in forested area Large down payment, fixed rate Insurance
Social	Divorce Death of spouse or family member	Always keep our relationship first Insurance
Transportation	Loss of mobility	Alternative transport Insurance

Gap Analysis

Gap analysis identifies the gaps between what you *want* to accomplish and what you can realistically achieve. Strategic plans for businesses or institutions frequently find that the plan for the future is great, but there is simply no way to fund everything in the plan. This happens to individuals as well. Look for gaps in each domain. Do you have the time, money, relationships, transportation or whatever else is needed to achieve what you have set out in your plan? If not, that is a gap, and you will have to find a way to close that gap.

The Gap analysis worksheet is designed to help you uncover any gaps in your plan and to find ways to close those gaps.

	Plan	Potential gap	Possible solution
Activities			
Finances			
Health			
Housing			
Social			
Transportation			

An example of Gap Analysis for a Young Adult.

	Plan	Potential gap	Possible solution
Activities			
Finances	Grad school	Tuition, books	Delay marriage, parents offered to provide
Health			
Housing	Housing during grad school	Rent	Delay marriage, parents will provide. Dorm?
Social	Marriage after college	Separation during grad school	Delay marriage till after grad school
Transportation			

Contingency Planning
(Chapter 19 in It's YOUR Future…)

What happens if one of your wild card scenarios occurs? Or the worst plausible scenario? Develop contingency plans to deal with these. "If…then" strategies are also helpful for contingency planning.

Wild card or Worst Plausible event	Strategy (__how__ will I deal with this event?)	Plan (what __actions__ will I take to deal with this?)

Use the strategy column to identify your general approach to dealing with this wild card or worst plausible event. Will you try to minimize, maximize, profit or avoid loss? For example, if you win the lottery, your strategy may be to avoid publicity and maximize the security of your winnings. In the Plan column, you can provide details for accomplishing your strategy.

For example, if your health fails (major stroke, Alzheimer's), and you become dependent on others, one strategy could be to enter an assisted living facility or a nursing home. The opposite strategy would be to avoid an institution and receive care at home.

Give each of these events serious thought. They may never occur, but if one of these events does happen, you'll be prepared.

In Conclusion...
(Chapter 20, 21 in It's YOUR Future...)

You have now explored your present and your future, created four future scenarios, designed a preferred future, devised strategies to achieve your preferred future, and developed an action plan to take you to that preferred future. You have also considered contingencies and should be prepared to make adjustments to your plan if that becomes necessary. The next, most important step is very simple: Start following your action plan and working toward your preferred future. Enjoy the benefits of your plan!

Live your plan!

After you have completed your workbook, wait a day or two, then review what you have done. You accomplished a lot completing this workbook, now reflect on what you have done and decide what you can do to improve your plan. Re-evaluate your strategies, your action plan, and your contingency plan. What did you leave out? What do you want to change? Go ahead. Make changes and improvements. This is your plan.

In six months or a year, look over your plan again. What has changed in your life that affects your plan? What outside forces are affecting your plan? Are you making progress? Is a different scenario unfolding than you expected? Adjust your plan as necessary to deal with the changes, but keep moving toward your personal vision. You can even change or re-define your vision.

Monitor the changes in your life and the world over the years, and keep adjusting your plan whenever you feel that it is necessary. If no changes are needed, then just keep following and living your plan.

The Author

Verne Wheelwright earned a Master's degree in Studies of the Future at the University of Houston then, convinced that there was a need, began research in personal futures for his Ph.D. dissertation. This workbook and his recent award-winning (Association of Professional Futurists' 2012 "Most Important Futures Work") book, *It's YOUR Future...Make it a Good One!* are the direct result of that research.

Verne was convinced that the futures methods that have been so successful for businesses, governments and other organizations should work for individuals as well. During his research, he developed a step-by-step approach to teaching individuals how to organize information from their own lives, then apply futures methods to explore and prepare for their futures. His articles about personal futures

Verne Wheelwright, Ph.D.

 have appeared in professional journals and other publications worldwide. *It's YOUR Future...* has been translated into Spanish and Turkish, and will soon be available in other languages.

His broad background in international business and his travels to much of the world have provided Verne with a strong foundation for his personal futures research, and added an understanding of cultural and economic differences that affect people's lives.

Since writing the original version of this workbook, Verne has tested it in presentations and workshops with people of different ages and varied cultural backgrounds, with gratifying results. He continues to receive compliments and expressions of gratitude from people who have attended his workshops, read his articles or visited his web site at www.personalfutures.net.

Verne plans to continue research, speaking, and writing about personal futures, and is encouraging futurists around the world to help people change their lives with personal futures workshops and training. He has created a web site for his books at www.vernewheelwright.com. Verne also writes a blog at www.wfs.org/blogs/verne-wheelwright. You can receive updates of his work on Twitter, @urfuturist or at the **Personal Futures Network** page on Facebook.

Verne and his wife live in Harlingen, Texas.

Acclaim for
It's YOUR Future... Make it a Good One!

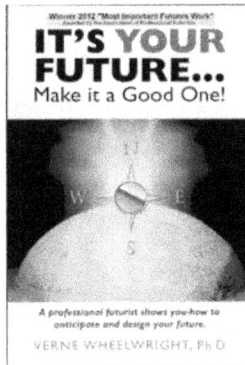

WINNER of 2012 "Most Important Futures Work"
Awarded by the Association of Professional Futurists

"In the introduction to his latest book... Wheelwright offers one of the most succinct explanations of the difference between prediction and foresight."
                                                    Joe Tankersley, "Unique Visions" blog.

"It's Your Future..."highly recommended. It's a reference manual for a lifetime.
                                                    Don Clifford, Author, *Ben Solomon*.

"...particularly useful for young professionals who are facing a multitude of choices in their career."
                                                    Marcel Bullinga, Author, *Welcome to the Future Cloud*.

"It's all here with charts and diagrams...but more than that it's a remarkably concise picture of the obstacles that serious people encounter when trying to organize their lives."
                                                    Mona D. Sizer, Author, *The Glory Guys*.

"Using *It's YOUR Future... Make it a Good One!* as a text in class again was a big success."
                                                    Dr. Roy Pearson, William & Mary's Mason School of Business.

"This book offers insights into how futures methods work and is intended to help individuals develop a long term perspective not only in their personal lives but also in their careers. The book is written to be useful to people of all ages, from teenagers to octogenarians."
                                                    Steve Saenz, Copernicus Radio.